103851

Wetlands

by Elizabeth Ring • Photographs by Dwight Kuhn

BLACKBIRCH PRESS
An imprint of Thomson Gale, a part of The Thomson Corporation

Detroit • New York • San Francisco • San Diego • New Haven, Conn. • Waterville, Maine • London • Munich

© 2005 Thomson Gale, a part of the Thomson Corporation.

Thomson and Star Logo are trademarks and Gale and Blackbirch Press are registered trademarks used herein under license.

For more information, contact
The Gale Group, Inc.
27500 Drake Rd.
Farmington Hills, MI 48331-3535
Or you can visit our Internet site at http://www.gale.com

ALL RIGHTS RESERVED
No part of this work covered by the copyright hereon may be reproduced or used in any form or by any means—graphic, electronic, or mechanical, including photocopying, recording, taping, Web distribution or information storage retrieval systems—without the written permission of the publisher.

Every effort has been made to trace the owners of copyrighted material.

Photo Credits: Cover, all photos © Dwight Kuhn Photography except pp. 3, 24 © photos.com

---

LIBRARY OF CONGRESS CATALOGING-IN-PUBLICATION DATA

Ring, Elizabeth, 1920–
    Wetlands / by Elizabeth Ring.
        p. cm. — (Communities in nature)
Summary: Presents information on the animals, plants, and general characteristics of wetlands, also known as marshes or swamps.
Includes bibliographical references (p. 47).
    ISBN 1-4103-0315-2 (hardback : alk. paper)
    1. Wetlands—Juvenile literature. [1. Wetlands. 2. Wetland ecology. 3. Ecology.] I. Title
II. Series: Ring, Elizabeth, 1920– , Communities in nature.

QH87.3.R55 2005
578.768—dc22
                                                                                                                        2003019630

Printed in China
10 9 8 7 6 5 4 3 2 1

Introduction

When you visit a salt marsh or freshwater swamp, you find yourself in a very watery world. In a salt marsh, you stand hip deep in tall grasses that border the sea. In a cypress swamp, you walk or float through a forest of tall trees. In both kinds of wetlands, rustlings and splashes and all kinds of calls tell you wildlife is near. The quieter you are, the quicker you get to see the secret lives that all wetlands hide.

Raccoons often visit the salt marsh to hunt for crayfish and crabs.

In the
Salt Marsh

I can spend whole days in the salt marsh, looking and listening, and poking around. Here, close to the ocean shore, the watery marsh is part saltwater, part fresh. No waves reach in from the sea. The marsh water is calm. When you wade through the reeds and feel the sun on your back, you feel as if there's just you, the marsh, the air and the sky.

When I visit the salt marsh, I carry a net to catch little marsh creatures.

You can sniff the salt air. The sea is not in sight, but you know it is there. At high tide, the sea brings new salt water in. It mixes with fresh water that flows in from the land. It's a mix that does all the marsh animals good. The water is rich with two kinds of food—one kind from the ocean, another kind from the land. When the tide's high, you can float on a raft through the water lanes in the marsh. You can slip up on wildlife that won't hear you coming.

At low tide, you can wade through the cord grass that bends when you walk. You really need boots to go into the marsh. In places, the mud is so thick it can suck your shoes right off your feet. If you're out to catch crabs or fish—to get a good look at them, or maybe to eat—you need a fishing net. And you want a bucket close by—to put your catch in.

I bring a big bucket to put my catch in— to watch them up close for awhile.

Insects are all over the marsh—in all colors, sizes, and shapes. Plant hoppers feed on the cord grass that grows everywhere. They suck the juice out of the grass blades—and can actually kill off the grass. That's not always a bad thing. Too much cord grass in a marsh can choke up the space that animals and other plants need.

Plant hopper insects suck juice from the cordgrass that grows everywhere in the marsh.

I can't say I like full-grown mosquitoes much. They bite—the females, at least. Young mosquitoes, called larvae, are quite different, though. They look a bit like grown mosquitoes without wings or legs. They hang upside down just under the water. They stick their tube-like tails up in the air—and that's how they breathe. When they swim, they wiggle and swish their tails. In fact, they're called "wigglers" sometimes.

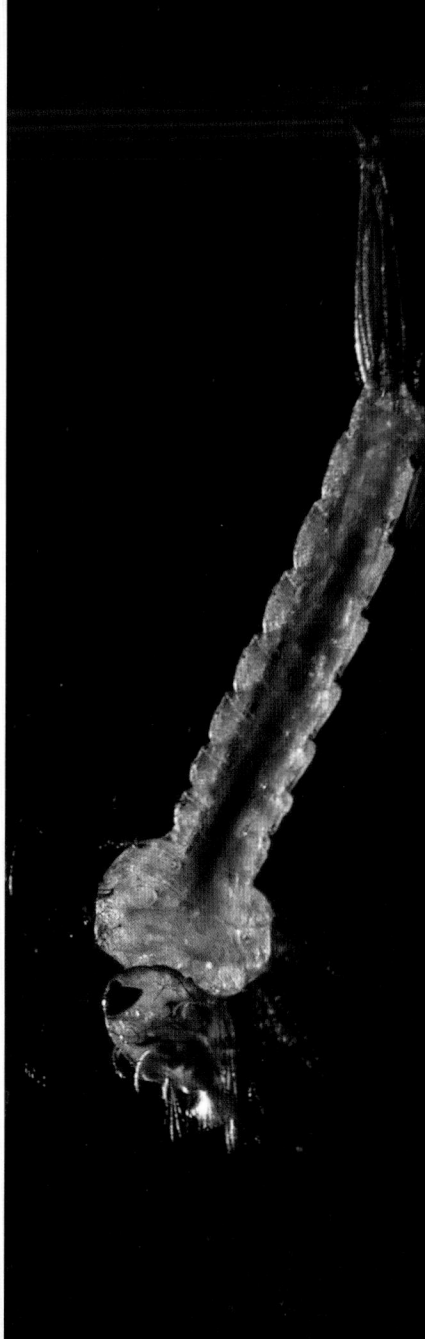

A young mosquito (a larva) sticks its tail up from the water to breathe air.

There's a green-headed horsefly. Just look at the size of its big striped eyes! Each eye has thousands of tiny lenses. Imagine the kind of pictures they see! Horseflies are pests—like mosquitoes, or worse. They bite hard. They especially pester horses. That's why they're called "horseflies"—even though they bite other animals, too. I wear bug-off lotion to keep all biting insects from feeding on me.

Horseflies look out through big striped eyes that are made up of thousands of lenses.

Down under the grass, in the water and mud, I always find lots of crabs. In fact, crabs can pinch your toes. That's another good reason to wear boots in the marsh! Blue crabs will eat almost anything they can find, dead or alive—fish, shrimp, oysters, clams, plants, even other blue crabs. A lot of people call the male blue crab "Jimmy." They call a female a "sook." I call them good to eat! So do herons and raccoons.

Opposite page: A blue crab gets ready to grab a shrimp or a clam with its fierce-looking claws.

Left: Hermit crabs have no shells of their own and have to borrow empty snail shells to live in.

There's a hermit crab crawling about. It is inside a snail shell, with just its walking legs and its claws sticking out. Hermit crabs don't live in shells of their own, the way other crabs do. As it grows, the crab has to keep looking for bigger and bigger homes to live in—until the crab is full grown.

Birds make nests in the marsh and roost (or rest) here for a while. I like the way a Merganser duck's feathers stick up from its skinny head. Merganser ducks dive for their food—insects and plants, but mostly fish. Their beaks have rough edges that hold slippery fish tight. When they want to fly, they have to run on the water and flap hard with their short wings—just to lift off. That's fun to watch.

Opposite page: A Merganser duck stares into the water before it dives in to catch a fish in its beak. Above: A great blue heron stands still as a statue, ready to stab a fish or crab with its sharp bill.

The great blue heron is a wading bird. It marches slowly through the marsh on its long stick legs. A great blue stands like a statue in one place, staring for a long time into the water. Then it darts its snaky neck out and stabs with its long, sharp beak. It comes up with a fish or a crab and swallows it whole. Herons don't have to run on the water before they can fly. They just spread their wide wings and lift off with a *whoooosh* and a squeaky cry.

The kingfisher is as good at waiting for lunch as a heron is. It sits on a tree branch at the marsh's edge. It just sits there and stares. It waits and waits. Suddenly, it will whiz into the air—and grab a dragonfly. It goes back to its perch and waits some more. Then it dives into the water and comes back up with a wriggling fish. Back again on its perch, it kills the fish, tosses it into the air, and catches it. Headfirst, the fish goes down whole.

This kingfisher has caught a big fish and carried it up to a tree branch to eat.

Little killifish are favorite meals for many creatures that live in the marsh. Herons and kingfishers gobble killifish up. Killifish themselves feed on worms, mosquito larvae, and bits of plants. Unless they are resting in some shady spot, they are quite hard to see. Groups of them, called "schools," dart this way and that— the way flocks of small birds swoop in the sky.

Killifish nibble on bits of plants as they hunt for mosquito larvae and worms.

One day, I stumbled across a busy raccoon. It had a big crab in its long-fingered paws. Raccoons are usually out hunting at night. You can hear them scream, sometimes two voices or three at a time. This one was on a daytime hunt, and it was really surprised to see me. But it just held that crab tight and stared up at me. I could tell that it wanted to eat, as if telling me to get lost. So I left the raccoon to its lunch.

A wary raccoon holds tight to a crab it has caught with its long-fingered paws.

I always discover things I've never seen before, when I go all the way through the marsh to the ocean shore. So many sea animals start their lives here that the salt marsh is called "the sea's nursery." It's a good place to grow up. That's true for me, too. I come here every year, to explore.

You never know what you'll find next in the tall marsh weeds that spread out to the sea.

In the Swamp

The swamp we visit is a mysterious place. The water lies flat, with hardly a ripple. Morning mists come and go—like ghosts drifting through the tall trees. There is barely a breeze in the steamy air. Sometimes we walk quietly on long wooden walkways that wind through the swamp. Sometimes we float in a silent flat-bottomed boat. No matter what path we take, we see swamp creatures doing what they do naturally—almost as if we aren't there.

A visit to the cypress swamp is like walking into a wet, ghostly woods.

Bald cypress trees grow right up out of the swamp. They look strong. Close to the water, their trunks spread out. The bulges are sometimes called "knees." Most trees that have needles keep their needles all year round, but not the bald cypress trees. Their branches get bare—or bald—in the fall. They drop their needles, just the way leafy trees drop their leaves.

In some trees, Spanish moss drips from branches. It looks to me like tangled gray hair. In fact, the moss was once called "Spanish beard." Some birds use the moss to line their nests. You see many insects and spiders crawling around in the moss.

Opposite page: Spanish moss hangs from the cypress trees, looking like long, gray, tangled witch hair.

Left: Fragrant water lilies smell sweet and make bright splashes of color all over the swamp.

Pink and white water lilies float on the water on their long, snaky stems. They smell so good that the word "fragrant" is part of their name. Their big, flat, green leaves make seats for insects. The leaves also make hiding places for swamp creatures below.

Like every animal in the swamp, crayfish are always searching for food. A crayfish swims around trees or walks around in the mud. It grabs its prey with its two claws like a crab's. It eats plants, fish, snails, insects, worms, even things that are dead. Of course, for other swamp creatures—fish, birds, and raccoons—the crayfish makes a tasty dish.

A crayfish feeds on a dead crayfish it has come upon—killed, perhaps, by a fish or a bird.

A small crayfish makes a good meal for a little blue heron. You can tell a little blue from a salt marsh's great blue heron by its smaller size. Also, its beak is not yellow, it's blue. Both kinds of herons stalk and strike at their prey. They stare hard at the water. Suddenly, they stab at the water and come up with some wiggling thing to eat.

Little blue herons feed in the swamp— just the way great blue herons hunt in the marsh.

Long-legged roseate spoonbills don't stab at their prey with their beaks. They swish their heads from side to side in the water to capture food with their bills shaped like spoons. Spoonbills are good parents. Both parents build a nest in a tree or a bush and care for their chicks until the young spoonbills can take care of themselves.

Just before dark is a good time to hear the hoots of a barred owl. The loud *hoo-hoo-hoo-HOOs* echo all over the swamp. If it's not too dark, you might catch sight of the bird itself. The marks on its feathers look like brown and white bars. You won't hear the owl fly as it dives on a mouse or a frog. Owls' wings don't make a sound.

Opposite page: Two spoonbill parents carefully guard the nest they both built for their chicks.

Right: A barred owl blinks itself awake, just before nightfall— when its hunt for mice begins.

Like owls, nutrias hunt for food mostly at night. Nutrias, though, eat only plants, not mice or frogs. They themselves have to watch out for hungry snakes, eagles, alligators, and owls. If you see a nutria, you might think it's a beaver or rat. Actually, they are all rodents, animals that gnaw. Like beavers, nutrias have to keep gnawing on plants. If they don't, their teeth grow too long for their mouths.

Nutrias wade through the swamp weeds, looking for juicy plants to eat.

Green anole lizards face each other on a branch, bobbing their head.

One day, I saw two green anole lizards on the branch of a tree. I wondered if they were both males. If so, I might get to see them bob their heads at each other, puff out pink throats, and start a fight. And if one was a female lizard and the other a male, a puffed-out pink throat might be the male asking the female to be his mate. But nothing happened at all, so I'll never know which was which.

Snapping turtles are fiercer than anole lizards. They have huge mouths, powerful jaws, and sharp, hooked beaks. To hunt, they hide in the mud and dart their heads out to snap at whatever comes by—insects, crayfish, smaller turtles, and fish. They eat plants and dead animals, too. About their only enemies are alligators.

Left: The snapping turtle looks fierce enough to snap your finger off—and it could.

Right: An alligator seems to smile a friendly grin, but it is not a friend to anything in the swamp.

An alligator is the most fearsome animal in the swamp. To me, it looks like a dinosaur. When it pokes its snout up through the weeds, it may look as if it is smiling. It's not. That's just the shape of its mouth. One time, we saw a big 'gator gliding along through the weeds. It hardly moved its huge head as it searched for something to eat—a turtle, fish, a snake, or maybe a nutria or raccoon. It even looked hard at us. We sort of stepped back on the walkway while we watched. Finally, the 'gator swam off—without making a ripple.

When a bullfrog shows up in the duckweed, its smile looks friendly enough to be real. Anyway, frogs are small. In the frog world, though, a bullfrog is a giant. It has a big deep voice to go with its big-frog size. On spring and summer nights you can hear the male bullfrogs booming *bum-a-BUM bum-a-BUM* all over the swamp. They are calling for a mate and to warn other males away from places they claim for themselves. Bullfrogs look fat and lazy, until you see one leap high on its springy back legs and snatch a fly out of the air with its long, sticky tongue.

The bullfrog wears a wide smile, but flies and other insects cannot call frogs their friends.

My little brother is good at catching frogs and toads. He likes to hold them, watch them, and make a new friend or two. One day, he borrowed my dad's big boots and caught a frog at the edge of the swamp. He held on with both hands (a frog has very slippery skin). We all looked into the frog's big bulgy eyes. We smiled back at the frog's smile. Then my brother held his hands open to let the frog go. Splash! It was gone, and the swamp was as quiet as it always seems to be—as if hardly anything at all is going on.

You can make friends with a bullfrog—if you can just hang onto its slippery skin.

More About Wetlands

Bald cypress trees

Alligators are lizard-like reptiles with long snouts and powerful tails. They have huge mouths and eighty teeth.

Bald cypress trees are tall, needle-leafed trees. Some are a thousand years old. Their bulgy "knees" are roots that rise above the swamp water.

Barred owls have sharp ears and eyes, and are good hunters. Pairs often mate for life and stay in their home territory for many years.

Blue crabs are large crabs. Their favorite meals are oysters and clams. They have many predators, including people.

Bullfrogs live along waterways, where there are many insects, spiders, worms, fish, tadpoles, and small snakes to eat.

Cord grass is a tough, long-leaved grass. It grows from 1 to 10 feet (0.3 to 3 m) tall, on mud and sand flats in salt marshes.

Crabs have hard shells, big claws, and jointed legs. They live in both salt marshes and inland freshwater wetlands.

Cord grass

Fragrant water lily

Crayfish look like little lobsters. They have hard shells, four pairs of walking legs, and two strong claws.

Fragrant water lilies are flowering plants that grow in swamps, lakes, streams, and ponds. Their sweet smell attracts many insects, which help pollinate the plants.

Great blue herons stand about 4 feet (1.2 cm) tall. They are the largest of American herons.

Green anoles are small, scaly lizards that feed on insects and spiders. They have sticky feet that keep them from falling off trees.

Hermit crabs twist themselves into the empty shells of sea animals, such as snails, to protect their soft bodies. They cling to the shells with their small hind legs.

Horseflies are also called "stouts" or "gadflies." Green horseflies are sometimes called "green-headed monsters."

Killifish are small fish, from 2 to 3.5 inches (5 to 9 cm) long. They are sometimes called "minnows," "mummies," or "chubs."

Kingfishers are long-billed birds that hunt in rivers, streams, and marshes for fish, insects, and frogs.

Killifish

Merganser duck

Little blue herons have long beaks and legs. They feed on fish, frogs, lizards, snakes, turtles, and crayfish.

Merganser ducks are handsome diving birds. They are often called "sawbills" because of the saw-like edges on their beaks.

Mosquitoes are insects related to flies. "Mosquito" means "little fly" in Spanish.

Nutrias (called "coypu" in Spanish) have soft fur and webbed hind feet. They are often prey to snakes, eagles, alligators, and owls.

Plant hoppers in a tidal marsh feed mostly on cord grass. They are also called "leaf hoppers."

Raccoons are land animals that often hunt food in wetlands. They can climb and swim.

Roseate spoonbills are pink-feathered wading birds that are sometimes mistaken for flamingoes, They often nest in flocks, among ibises, herons, and egrets.

Salt marshes are wetlands near the ocean shore. They are a mixture of fresh water and salt water. Many land and sea animals start their lives in the tidal waters.

Snapping turtles, like other turtles, have two hard shells that cover their soft bodies. The top shell is called a carapace. The bottom shell is called the pastron.

Snapping turtle

Spanish moss

Spanish moss grows in mossy strands on trees, but does not harm trees by feeding on them. Instead, it draws its moisture and nutrients from the air.

Swamps are shallow, muddy, freshwater wetlands. As in salt marshes, hundreds of animals give birth and raise their young in and around swamps.

Wetlands are places where water covers the ground most of the time. Marshes, swamps, and bogs are all wetlands.

For More Information

Life in a Wetland by Allan Fowler (Children's Book Press, 1999)

Marshes and Swamps by Ron Hirschi (Delacorte, 1994)

Salt Marsh by Paul Fleisher (Marshall Cavendish, 1999)

Swamp by Donald M. Silver (McGraw Hill, 1997)

Wetlands: All About Bogs, Bayous, Swamps, and a Salt Marsh or Two by Vicki Leon (Silver Burdett Press, 1998)

Wild and Swampy by Jim Arnosky (HarperCollins, 2000)

www.epa.gov/owow/wetlands
Kinds of wetlands, their functions, values, and wildlife. (U.S. Environmental Protection Agency)

www.nwf.org/wetlands
Kinds of wetlands, their types, benefits, and wildlife. (National Wildlife Federation)

Index

alligators, 36, 37, 40, 44
anole lizard, 35, 42

bald cypress trees, 25, 40
barred owl, 33, 40
birds, 14–17, 30–33, 40, 43, 44, 45
blue crabs, 12, 41
blue heron, 15, 30–31, 42, 44
bullfrog, 38–39, 41

cord grass, 7, 8, 41, 44
crabs, 12–13, 21, 41, 43
crayfish, 28–29, 42
cypress trees, 25, 40

duck, 14, 44
duckweed, 38

fish, 14, 17, 18–19, 43
flowers, 27, 42
frog, 38–39, 41

grasses, 3, 7, 8, 41, 44
great blue heron, 15, 42

green–headed horsefly, 10–11, 43

hermit crab, 13, 43
heron, 15, 17, 30–31, 42, 44
horsefly, 10–11, 43
hunting, 21, 36, 43

insects, 8–11, 26, 27, 42, 44

killifish, 18–19, 43
kingfisher, 16–17, 43

larvae, 9
little blue heron, 30–31, 44
lizards, 35, 42

Merganser duck, 14, 44
mosquitoes, 9, 44

nests, 14, 26
nutria, 34, 44

owl, 33, 40, 44

pests, 10
plant hoppers, 8, 44
plants, 26, 42, 46
prey, 28, 44

raccoon, 20–21, 45
reptile, 40
rodents, 34
roseate spoonbills, 32, 45

salt marsh, 3, 4–19, 41, 45, 46
snapping turtle, 36, 45
Spanish moss, 26, 46
spiders, 26
spoonbill, 32, 45
swamp, 3, 24–39, 46

tides, 5–7
trees, 3, 25, 40
turtles, 36, 45

water lilies, 27, 42